The
illusion
of
control

steven wiese

with Sharon M. Knudson

CROWN
IMPERIAL
PRESS

Published by Crown Imperial Press, 21211 Imperial Ave. N., Forest Lake, MN 55025, tel.: 651-464-1121.

Cover and interior design by Sheryl Thornberg.

Printed in the United States of America.

ISBN 13: 978-0-615-22104-5

Acknowledgments

My friend, colleague, and mentor, the late Dr. William Backus, taught me how to apply the Misbelief Therapy approach he developed, used, and wrote about for many years. This book is an extension of his work, and I am especially grateful for his influence and teaching.

I also want to acknowledge the many clients who allowed me to use this material in its early stages and who gave me feedback. I've found that some of the most courageous people in the world come through the doors of our Counseling Center to tackle problems and issues known only to them and their counselor.

A special thank you goes to the people who reviewed early versions of this material, including the client I call "Margie;" my father and mother, Roger and Marilyn Wiese; my wife Sherry; and my daughter Caitlin.

I'm grateful to Sharon M. Knudson, whose careful polishing of my sometimes cumbersome prose makes me look like a better writer than I am.

The look of the finished product is reflective of the creative talents of Gayle Aldrich and Sheryl Thornberg who work in the Resource Ministries of North Heights. Thank you also to Jessie Nilo for providing the graphic diagrams for these pages.

Finally, many thanks to my colleagues at The Center for Christian Psychological Services and to the lay counselors of The Counseling Clinic at North Heights Lutheran Church, both in St. Paul, Minnesota. Because you challenged me during our supervision and staff meetings, to clearly communicate and then write about these ideas, they can now be more widely used to benefit those people who suffer relentlessly under the Illusion of Control.

Introduction

Are you a perfectionist who blames yourself whenever things work out less than 100 percent right?

Are you constantly telling yourself, "If only I would have done x or y, everything would be fine," or, "Things would be okay if I had just said/done/thought/prayed the right thing..."

Are you finding yourself increasingly depressed, with a profound sense of failure?

Have you tried to work on your problems, perhaps even with a counselor, but seem to get stuck when you try to let yourself off the hook?

Are you troubled by all the problems surrounding you, no matter how little you've contributed to them?

If so, you may be living with the Illusion of Control.

Chapter 1

M argie (not her real name) had been doing counseling
with me for over a year. Diligent, hard-working, and
bright, she was a client who did the difficult work of
trying to get better.

We had worked through some severe childhood trauma,
had discussed at length her family of origin, and had applied the
tools of Misbelief Therapy throughout—that is, we used the
approach Dr. William Backus had developed and written about
in a series of books starting with *Telling Yourself the Truth*.
Margie had journalled her self-talk, watched for the lies she was
telling herself, and worked hard to replace the lies with
Truth—that is, Truth from Scripture and from common sense.

Yet, she suffered. Yes, some things changed.... She escaped
from an abusive husband who was unwilling to change. She got
over some of the doubts about her abilities and went back to finish college. She worked on her parenting skills and helped her
children cope with the dysfunction in their family while pointing
them to the Lord. Still, there was trouble.

Both of us were grateful when the Lord, through the work
and the trust relationship we'd built up, revealed a central, key
misbelief that she held to be absolutely true:

"I am the problem."

Margie's reasons for carrying this misbelief around for
decades were many. She was always *the odd one out* in her family. They treated her differently than they treated anyone else,
and everyone seemed to go along with what she perceived as
unhealthy patterns of interaction. She even remembered a key
incident in her childhood when her older brother had looked at
her with disgust and said,

"This family was fine until you were born."

So Margie and I began looking at the misbelief. For a cognitive behavioral psychologist like me, this was like a miner striking the mother lode of gold ore. Now we could integrate the entire truth from Scripture, from her other experiences, from logic and common sense, and work on changing this depressing misbelief. I had confidence that within a few weeks, maybe a bit longer, she would be dramatically improved!

I was wrong.

Margie was able to look at what was true from Scripture:

- *"For I know the plans I have for you," declares the Lord, "plans to prosper you and not to harm you, plans to give you hope and a future"* (Jeremiah 29:11).

- *"We are God's workmanship, created in Christ Jesus to do good works, which God prepared in advance for us to do"* (Ephesians 2:10).

Margie could look logically at her family history: the presence of chronic mental illness, personality disorders, post-traumatic stress disorder from Vietnam and perhaps going back as far as World War II, and childhood sexual abuse—all taking place in the context of an apparently Christian, church-going family.

But for some reason, Margie simply couldn't, or wouldn't, accept the Truth and change her misbelief.

Obviously she wasn't resistant to change per se. And she was certainly intelligent enough to understand the truth, and the dissonance between it and her misbelief. But she seemed unable to change it.

I wish I could still remember the exact way in which we gained the important insight that finally unlocked her healing and started me on a journey to understand the Illusion of Control. But I can't.

What I do know is that it struck me in its utter power and simplicity: "This is her solution."

Chapter 2

Ｐeople come to me with their problems. They come because they're depressed, anxious, or angry. They have problems with spouses, children, bosses, employees. They have problems with their churches, with their pastors. Sometimes they come to me because they're in grieving. But everyone comes with problems—and they're looking for solutions.

In reality, my job is often to help people find the tools with which they can solve their own problems rather than solve them for them. Counseling isn't like going to the doctor for a prescription—it only works when people will make changes. They need to change behavior, beliefs, jobs, relationships. Often my role is to be a facilitator of that change. Nevertheless, when people work on their problems, more often than not we find the solutions with God's help and guidance.

So what would I do with Margie? I was faced with the reality that I was trying to help her by defining the problem and trying to find her new solutions. The problem? Her deep-seated belief that in her family, in her lost marriage, and in her relationships with both people and God, *she* was the problem.

I applied all the tools at my disposal to help her change that misbelief. I expected to solve her problem, but I ran into this brick wall:

That which I defined as her problem was functioning as her solution.

This insight itself was not necessarily new. After all, we regularly tell people that their solutions are actually problems. The drinker who uses alcohol to avoid emotions is using it as a solution to his emotional problems. The gambler who keeps going to the casino to solve her debt problem sees the gambling as a solution, not the problem. And, as I recalled from a case years before, a bulimic teenager sees her problem as her weight, while a therapist, or for that matter, pretty much anyone who cares about her, sees her binging and purging as the problem. It was a comment from just such a bulimic teen that set me up for understanding Margie.

Several years before, a teenage girl I was working with reported to me that her boyfriend had given her an ultimatum: he cared about her so much that unless she would commit to not making herself vomit, he couldn't stay with her. He couldn't watch her kill herself that way. She agreed to try. Several weeks went by and I met again with her.

"Well, how is it going?" I asked.

She sighed and said, "Oh, all right I guess. I decided that my boyfriend was right—so I haven't vomited for three weeks."

"That's great!" I exclaimed, pleased with such a great solution to her problem. Then, she said something that changed my perspective completely.

"But you know, Steve," she said, and paused. She looked down at her hands, then back at me. "You know, I really miss it...."

I was stunned. Not being a bulimic myself, I could only understand the clinical perspective rather than the subjective experience. I couldn't fathom vomiting (something I dread whenever I'm sick) as something that could actually be missed. But that girl taught me a very important therapeutic lesson:

> **Sometimes, what we define as the client's *problem*
> may for the client be such a significant *solution*
> that they are very resistant to giving it up—
> and when they do, they may actually *miss*
> "the problem."**

So for this young woman struggling with bulimia, she was being asked to give up her solution without having a viable, tangible alternative. She gave it up in the interest of maintaining her relationship with her boyfriend. But as she so poignantly said, she wasn't glad to be rid of the "problem"—rather, she missed it!

It was this experience I recalled while listening to Margie's struggle. I began to ask myself, and eventually Margie, this question:

How could the core belief, "I am the problem," somehow be a solution?

Looking back on it now, just posing the question brings understanding. Margie didn't take too long to figure it out either.

"Well, Steve, it's pretty obvious, isn't it?" she said. "If I can find a way to label *myself* as the problem, there is hope—some possibility that I can make adjustments and make the outcome favorable. In other words, If I'm the problem, I'm the solution!"

There we have the basic misbelief at the heart of the Illusion of Control:

"If I'm the problem, then I'm the solution."

This insight helped considerably in understanding the problem—but we needed to understand more fully how this could be a solution that was so resistant to change, even in the face of powerful evidence to the contrary. Here we need to look at some additional background from Margie's life experience.

Chapter 3

At one point, Margie summarized part of her belief system this way:

"The way it ran through my mind as a child was like this:
If I were bright enough, or good enough,
I wouldn't find myself in these situations.
I can never see it coming—but if I could,
I would do something about it.
Then they'd love me and care about me
and accept me."

As Margie and I talked about her family life when she was growing up, I began to think of other clients whose stories, while not exactly the same, had certain general features in common with hers. The specific dysfunction or psychopathology that existed in those families included alcoholism, drug abuse, physical or sexual abuse, severe chronic mental illness, anger, and rage with emotional or verbal abuse. Some families had religious beliefs or practices that were very disturbing or hurtful. Regardless of the specifics, I began to see these characteristics frequently present:

1. My client had experienced family life as chaotic and unpredictable.
2. For my client, family life was physically, emotionally, and/or spiritually painful.
3. A legalistic or works-oriented church or family religious experience was often present.
4. The client received the message (either directly like Margie, or more indirectly) that they were to blame for the family's ills. Either that, or over time they came to that conclusion for themselves.

1. The person had experienced family life as chaotic and unpredictable.

In his book, *The Relaxation Response,* Herbert Benson says we experience stress whenever our environment demands that we make a behavioral adaptation. In other words, when our life circumstances or environment changes and in some way requires a response from us, we experience stress.[1]

If we keep that concept in mind and consider a chaotic and unpredictable family, we can see that minute by minute, hour by hour, day by day, life is stressful. The child growing up in this environment must constantly be on guard, waiting for the next turn of events to unfold that will rock their world.

- Will Daddy yell at me? Will Mom?
- Will Mom get drunk again tonight?
- Will I get hit again today?
- Will Mom's boyfriend make a pass at me?

This kind of environment creates an overwhelming sense of victimization and of feeling trapped in circumstances beyond the child's control. John Gottman refers to the resulting emotional experience as "Diffuse Physiological Arousal," and notes that it affects children and adults alike, emotionally as well as physically. Human beings simply cannot thrive in this kind of environment.[2]

2. For my client, family life was physically, emotionally, and/or spiritually painful.

- You're twelve years old, and your father breaks your jaw with the cast on his broken wrist.
- You are five years old and your brother sexually molests you.
- You're nine years old and have to cook for your siblings again because your mother is passed out on the bathroom floor.
- You're thirteen years old and while you're out riding your bike, you discover your father with another woman.

- You are told that from your conception, your mother considered you a mistake. It's no wonder she treats you like one.
- You're told, "This family was fine until you were born."
- You're told, "You'll never amount to anything—in fact, you're retarded."
- You are taken to church regularly, but your family's behavior at church is dramatically at odds with the abusive world of your home life. *The rock of the church* has a rocky marriage at home, and the one who raises his voice in praise on Sunday morning raises his voice in criticism all week.
- You go to dinner at your grandparents' house. After eating several bites of "turkey," you're informed (with great laughter all around) that you're actually eating your pet goose.

Of course, the list could go on and on with stories that are even worse. Yet other stories might be less dramatic but devastating in their own way, such as a father giving his teenage daughter a nickname that has sexual overtones.

In each of these situations, the environment in which the child grows up is not only unpredictable and chaotic— it inflicts a significant amount of pain as well.

3. A legalistic or works-oriented church or family religious experience was often present.

Among Christians, it is frequently the case where their family belongs to a denomination or group whose theology is fairly legalistic and rigid. In particular, there is a focus on the *don'ts* of Scripture rather than on grace and forgiveness. Sometimes it's the microculture of the family that interprets their religious understanding in this way even though the church's teaching may not be quite as extreme.

Please note: I'm not suggesting that we ignore explicit biblical guidelines regarding our behavior. Clearly, there is a place for the Law in guiding our daily lives. However, when Christians start to think like Pharisees, there can be a problem.

Sometimes a huge amount of love and acceptance can be expressed in even strict families. It's only when there's a lack of warmth, or when there's actual, abusive behavior (as in the examples mentioned above) that, combined with legalism, the person growing up in that environment pays a huge price.

What these people begin to believe is that there is a direct, one-to-one relationship between their behavior and God's love and acceptance. Rather than beginning from the Truth that "God is Love," they come to view God as a harsh judge who's waiting for people to mess up so He can punish them. They begin to believe things such as:

- Blessings from God are directly proportional to your behavior. If someone is suffering, it's because of some sin in their life.

- God answers prayers only when righteous, holy, *perfect* people pray. If you have any type of sin in your life, God won't listen to you.

- There is a right way, even a formulaic way, to pray. If you get it wrong, God ignores you.

- God ignores you if you haven't done the right spiritual exercises or disciplines. Are you tithing? Did you have a quiet time today? Are you going to church weekly, or more? Are you witnessing at every opportunity? Are you operating in God's perfect will?

Overall, these people believe and behave as if they were human *doings* rather than human *beings*. Their view of God is like that of a Santa Claus: "He sees you when you're sleeping, he knows when you're awake, he knows when you've been bad or good, so be good, for goodness sake!"

What these Christians are failing to realize is that the God of the Bible sent His Son "while we were yet sinners," as Paul writes. Jesus came to restore our relationship with God, the

Father. For too many, however, Christianity doesn't begin with God—it begins with people.

4. **The client received the message (either directly like Margie, or more indirectly) that they were to blame for the family's ills. Either that, or over time they came to that conclusion for themselves.**

- "You were an accident."

- "You destroyed my marriage."

- "I tried to abort you but failed."

- "I could have gone to college if it weren't for you being born."

- "Our family was fine until you came along."

- "Because of you, I had to get married."

These are just some examples of the kind of statements people hear from parents and siblings. Over time, these statements form the misbelief system the person carries with them into the rest of their life. This is the misbelief system that moves them into the worldview that says,

"I am the problem."

Not all families are as overt with their accusations as this, however. Sometimes, it's an overheard conversation that communicates the same message. Sometimes it's the discrepancy between what is given to the *favorite* child or children in contrast to what is given to the other. When Dad attends every game a son ever plays but pays no attention to the daughter's games or concerts, she'll naturally draw some conclusions. When *the golden child* is bragged about while another child is rarely mentioned, a message is communicated.

Children are constantly trying to make sense of their world. They also work to understand the rules and guidelines, culture and language of their family. They're very adept at this and will put the pieces together to form a coherent view of themselves and their family.

One day Margie told me about the infamous "lemon drop incident." She was at her grandparents' house, where her grandfather was in bed, gravely ill. Margie had been told to go outside and stay there. After a while, she sneaked into the kitchen to grab a lemon drop from the candy dish, but when she heard someone coming, she got scared and ran back out. The screen door slammed shut behind her with a bang! Her mother ran after her. "Be quiet!" she scolded. "Are you trying to *kill* your grandfather making noise like that?"

Later that afternoon, Margie's grandfather died. How did her young mind put the pieces together? Clearly there was only one possible conclusion. *She* had killed her grandfather!

Let me give you a rather benign example. I'm 5'11" tall—by all accounts, above average height for an American male. However, I grew up in a family in which my father was 6'7" tall! Most of my male cousins grew to be over 6' tall—all the way to 6'8". My brother is 6'4". Even my sister is 5'10"! What is a person to conclude when, as an adult, he still has to stand on tiptoes to give his father a hug?

Fortunately, in my family, the issue was moot. We joked about my father's height, but never anyone else's lack thereof. Still, I logically reached the conclusion, "I'm not particularly tall." How much more profound (and serious) when a child concludes, based on the information he gets from his environment, that he is an inferior member of his family!

Chaos and unpredictability, pain and hurt, rigid or works-oriented religion, actual or implied blame. These are the seeds that can be sown in a child's belief system that ultimately lead to the Illusion of Control.

Chapter 4

Why do these things set people up for accepting the Illusion of Control? Let's look a bit more closely at what happens in a child who grows up in this environment.

- They live in a world that could cause them emotional or physical pain at any moment.

- They need to become keen observers of the human behavior all around them.

- They are usually told that they are the problem, and over time, they accept the diagnosis.

- And they begin to hold on to that misbelief with unbelievable tenacity.

Why? Because it gives them hope.

"Right," you might be saying. "I can see where it might give them depression and anxiety, but hope?"

Yes, hope. Here's how.

With this situation, there's always the possibility that they'll actually succeed in getting things right: saying the right thing, doing the right thing, praying the right thing, or avoiding the right thing. Someday they might just have everything come together perfectly, and they'll beat the system! After all, if they're the problem, they're also the solution. This is the hope: that they'll succeed in getting it so right that they'll solve it all—the chaos and the pain—for all time... or at least they'll be able to get it right and prevent the chaos and the pain for a moment or in a given situation.

This hope is powerful—so powerful that people will hold onto the Illusion of Control for many, many years. Given the choice between unpredictable pain or even the remotest possibility of escaping the plight of a victim, they choose the latter.

This is illustrated in the extreme in the stories of hostages and prisoners of war. When prisoners are randomly beaten and tortured, it often becomes easy to get them to do or say things that they'd never do or say in other circumstances. Their captors give them the hope that by cooperating, they'll reduce their unpredictable pain. Indeed, the heroic stories of people like Admiral John Stockdale demonstrate how challenging it is not to give in to this Illusion. Stockdale spent nearly eight years imprisoned in North Vietnam after being shot down, and four of those years were in solitary confinement. Throughout his ordeal, he refused to cooperate with his captors. People like Admiral Stockdale are amazing precisely because they endured the random and unpredictable pain for years without being tempted to give in and gain the Illusion of Control their captors offered.

Here is another, less serious example. I've always been intrigued with what seems to be a high frequency of superstitious behavior among major league baseball players and their fans. We see rally caps worn upside down, pre-game meals and rituals, fans wearing certain types of clothing, ritualistic ways of preparing to bat. Why? Part of the explanation is that even the best major league batters fail more times at the plate than they succeed. The benchmark batting average of all time is .406 by Ted Williams in 1941. Recent batting champions (the best batters in the majors) have succeeded at the plate only about 35 out of every 100 attempts! Given how painful it is to strike out or get put out, and because it's a relatively unpredictable event, I believe the players try to find some means of gaining the Illusion of Control. So if they got a hit wearing their red boxers, they might wear their red boxers to every game until their "luck" changes.

Let me illustrate further. Former Red Sox and Yankees player Wade Boggs was often referred to as "Chicken Man" because he habitually ate chicken before every game. He'd also start wind sprints exactly 16 minutes before each game. Frank Viola, a three-time Major League Baseball All-Star and former

Cy Young Winner, had a secret to his success on the mound. He'd clean the mound before every inning, kicking up dirt exactly four times. However, if something bad happened, he wouldn't do it in repetition of fours anymore. Instead, he'd try threes or fives.

These are relatively innocuous examples, but they illustrate how tempting it is to look for Control in painful and unpredictable circumstances. By performing the rituals, the potential "victim" summons hope. And as I said earlier, if given a choice between having to endure unpredictable pain or entertaining even a remote possibility they might not wind up as a failure (victim), people often choose the latter.

There is, however, a big problem. Since the control people seek is only an illusion, the approach simply cannot work. So after years of trying, most of these people come to an inevitable conclusion:

"I am a failure."

And having reached that conclusion, their emotional life often spirals into a dark hole called depression.

Chapter 5

It's a typical day at my clinic office, and my appointment schedule shows a new patient. This is a 42-year-old woman who's seeking help. When I call her name, she moves slowly down the hall and into my office. She looks flat and beaten-down—she looks depressed. Now faced with the first difficult decision of this hour, she turns to me with a look of vague anxiety and asks, "Where do you want me to sit?" She's unable to decide for herself if she should sit in the recliner or on the couch. She needs guidance even for that.

As her story unfolds, I hear that she's feeling utterly hopeless and defeated. She feels like a failure as a wife, a mother, and a Christian. She exhibits other depression symptoms as well: she's having trouble sleeping, has lost weight, and can't concentrate. She's not at all optimistic about her future and sees no real hope for change. It doesn't take me long to conclude that she's another victim of the Illusion of Control.

What I've noticed over the years is that people can manage their lives by using the worldview that they are the solution to their problems for a relatively long period of time. But almost inevitably there comes a time, often in their thirties or forties, when the collective weight of all their apparent failures finally weighs them down and overwhelms any sense of hope they had gained from looking at life with the Illusion of Control.

There seem to be several reasons for this. First, remember how powerful hope can be! The Illusion of Control gives them this hope for a time. But along with the hope comes a terrible burden—it's all up to them. They are the key, the critical variable in their worldview.

Second, these are often people who are extremely honest and truthful. They want to do the right thing, of course, but they also want to be brutally honest in their self-evaluation.

While even the best of people have problems and struggles in their lives, these people look at their problems, mistakes, and failures with excruciating honesty. In fact, they keep track of all of their shortcomings. Then, after running this experiment for a while, they come to the inevitable conclusion that they have clearly failed. Not only that, but given the assumptions they're operating under (that is, the Illusion of Control), they think they're telling themselves the truth! That's why this is so difficult to argue against using traditional Cognitive Behavioral approaches. Both on the surface and personally within themselves, they're being utterly honest.

Third, this becomes even more serious if they encounter difficult people or situations. It could be members of their family or in their work situation. It might be a child who does poorly in school or is a behavior problem. It could be that their marriage is struggling. Situations like these serve to magnify their sense of failure. To them, this becomes profound failure, and the distress is that much worse.

What I find is that these people eventually come in like the 42-year-old woman did, feeling defeated and depressed. They exhibit the classic Depressive Triad of depression self-talk:

1. I'm no good.

2. My life is no good.

3. My future is hopeless.

In addition, they complain of anxiety. After all, they're back to square one. They've been trying for years to prevent the pain, and it hasn't worked. Now they're really worried about what might happen to them. Based on their experience, they're predicting something bad will happen again, they'll fail again, and that will lead to an awful catastrophe.

Chapter 6

O ver the years, as I applied this model in therapy, I tried
several ways to summarize it with clients. After some trial
and error, and with input from clients (often my best
source of good ideas), I came to use the following diagram to
illustrate their world to them: this is the Illusion of Control.

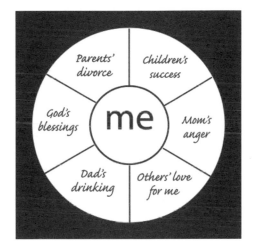

The worldview that I call the Illusion of Control puts *me* in
the center of the world. Unlike pride and narcissism, this is not
because I'm so wonderful. Instead, it is a functional position;
that is, it indicates that all the other factors and elements in my
life revolve around and depend on me for their outcome and
incidence. It illustrates the profound misbelief that *I am the
problem* (and therefore, the solution). It needs to be personalized
for each individual, but the general pattern is illustrated here.

These people have concluded that the painful things in their
lives, such as Mom's anger, Dad's drinking, a divorce, or the
abuse they are experiencing, hinge on them. It is up to *them* to

do whatever they need to do to make sure Mom stays calm, Dad stays sober, the folks stay together, or their brother stops being abusive. When these things don't happen, they blame themselves, sometimes in vague terms such as, "I just didn't do enough," or "I need to be more godly." Or they blame themselves in more specific terms such as, "I need to be more patient so Dad will stay calm," or, "I need to be an A student so my parents will stay together," or, "Even if I'm responsible for only 1% of the problem, if I changed my 1%, they might not treat me so poorly."

As a counselor, my initial goal in showing clients this worldview is to test the hypothesis. I don't tell them, "This is how you see the world." Rather, I lay everything out in the context of the history they have presented to me, with their particular hurts and fears identified in the sections of the diagram.

These hurts and fears include things such as:

- Their parents' divorce.

- A parent's drinking or drug use.

- Parental suicide, or even murder/suicide.

- Physical, sexual, emotional abuse of the client or other family members.

  Note: In many kinds of abuse, the perpetrator specifically tells the child that if they tell someone, terrible things will happen to them or other members of the family. The perpetrator places the victim precisely in the middle of the Illusion of Control model.

- General family dysfunction.

- The death of a family member (recall Margie's lemon drop story).

- Leaving a particular church.

- Their parents' anger, depression, or other serious mental health problem.

- Parental abandonment.

- Parental rejection.

- God's apparent lack of love or protection.

- God's apparently deaf ear when it came to prayer.

- Lack of healing or protection for a loved one, even when prayed for.

When Bob was growing up, he was the youngest of several brothers. For the most part, he wasn't physically abused by his father, but he witnessed beatings to his brothers so severe that he came to the conclusion that it was only a matter of time until it would happen to him. He decided he had to do whatever he could to prevent it.

As a result, Bob began to develop his worldview, and when I met him in middle age, he was depressed and anxious about many things, particularly his work life. He was incredibly stressed, keenly aware of making sure he did everything right and on time. His boss was notorious for heaping on work and deadlines beyond any reasonable expectation, and became extremely upset with people when they didn't perform at the level of his expectations.

Bob worked long hours, on weekends, and even during vacations when deadlines were looming. But he constantly came up short. He was more and more sure that he was a failure at work, always anxious about the severe response he might soon get from the boss. Bob was living in his version of the Illusion of Control, and he was overwhelmed.

If you're reading this and have wondered if the Illusion of Control might apply to you, take a moment and write down those things that, based on your own life experience, would be in your worldview.

- What have you been telling yourself you are responsible for?

- Do you seem to place yourself in the center of the world,

hoping you can save it and yourself from the chaotic, painful circumstances around you?

Fill in the diagram below. This is your personal model of the Illusion of Control. Remember that you may have developed this worldview to give you hope in a chaotic, unpredictable, and painful set of circumstances. You grabbed hold of it because you believed that if you were the problem, you could be the solution!

My World
(my Illusion of Control)

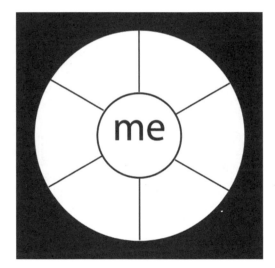

Chapter 7

W hen my client Margie and I began to understand the nature of her Illusion of Control, we knew it had to be dealt with effectively if she was going to move ahead in her healing. That presented me with a new problem: "How do you get someone to give up a solution that is also a core problem?"

I began looking at how we counselors do this in simpler situations. If a client solves anxiety problems by avoiding anxiety-producing situations, he's given strategies to relax and reduce anxiety. Soon he's able to do what he was afraid to do previously. Likewise, if a woman eats in order to soothe herself, she's given alternative strategies that reduce stress but don't cause weight gain—such as exercise.

In these situations, we don't just ask the person to give up what they're doing, we *replace* their unhealthy solutions with alternative solutions that are healthy and truth-based. People won't give up a known, unhealthy solution for the unknown. But they will give up a known, unhealthy solution for a clear, understandable one—even if it involves risk. Often, by this time, they're so ready to feel good again that the risk of change is preferable to the cost of repeating what they've done for years. Their hopelessness becomes the motivator for gaining hope through a new strategy.

Luke tells such a story in Chapter 8 of his Gospel. As Jesus makes his way through a crowd, a woman moves toward him. She's trying to stay hidden but wants to get close enough to touch his cloak. She's risking the wrath of the teacher, Jesus, and possibly that of her community for having the audacity to touch a man in this way. She's desperate—she's been bleeding for twelve years and has tried every possible solution without success. She finally succeeds in touching Jesus' garment, and hopes to disappear into the crowd. Luke finishes the story this way: *But Jesus said, "Some one touched me; for I perceive that power has gone forth from me." And when the woman saw that she was not hidden, she came trembling, and falling down before him declared in the presence of all the people why she had touched him, and how she had been immediately healed. And he said to her "Daughter, your faith has made you well; go in peace"* (Luke 8:46–48 RSV).

For her, the risk of change (trying something new) was preferable to doing the same thing over and over. And, in her case, it was a miraculous change indeed.

Margie was like this woman. She had had enough of all the old, failing strategies she had employed. She was ready to give up the old and try something new, even if it was risky.

The question I had to answer was, "What is the alternative strategy I can offer her?"

I also knew that the solution would have to be the Truth.

Chapter 8

O
ver time, I developed a clearer, alternative model using three categories: Control, Influence, and Concern. This model represents the way things really are in our life experience and in our world. And it allows us to consider our choices within that world.

Control: There are some aspects of our lives over which we have total control (at least from a human perspective). That is, we are the only person with the responsibility and authority to accomplish some things. For example, what we choose to eat is under our control. Whether we get up when our alarm rings in the morning is under our control. The words we speak to our spouses or children are under our control. How we vote in an election is under our control.

Influence: There are circumstances in our lives in which we have some level of influence but not total control. The level of influence may vary from quite a lot to very little. For example, I have influence over my wife's emotions. If I ignore her in the morning and speak critically to her during the day, or even worse, forget her birthday or an anniversary, my behavior will definitely influence her mood. However, I will never have total *control* over her mood because there are other influences in her life as well. How is she feeling physically? What were some of the positive things that happened during her day that might make my foolishness less of a factor? If she had a fabulous day, my thoughtlessness might not bring her down at all. If, on the other hand, she had a terribly difficult day, even a small amount of criticism from me could have a huge impact.

Concern: There are some things in our lives over which we have neither *control* nor *influence*, which nevertheless affect us in some way. For example, I live in Minnesota, where spring weather can vary from a low of 35 degrees to a high of over 75. Morning radio programs joke about how difficult it is to decide which items of clothing to have in storage and what to have available for use. When it comes to the weather in Minnesota, all we can do as human beings is adjust to the circumstances. While we can *control* what we wear and *influence* our children to dress appropriately, there is nothing we can do to change the weather.

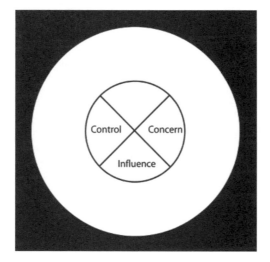

These three categories are extremely important to understand. This is the beginning of the model that can be used to challenge the Illusion of Control in which we think everything in our world is under our control.

The first step is to begin to recognize and accurately assign situations in your life to one of the three categories. Many times, the failure to understand the true nature of our control or influence (or lack thereof) is what creates stress and relationship problems in our lives.

Here are some examples of situations in which you would have control, influence, or concern. Read through each one and identify which category would apply.

Control, Influence, or Concern?

1. Your six-year-old daughter won't get out of bed in the morning.

2. Your sixteen-year-old son, who is six feet tall, weighs 155 pounds, and is stronger than you, his mother, won't get out of bed in the morning.

3. You love ice cream, but you need to lose ten pounds. You're looking into the freezer at a five-quart pail of luscious vanilla....

4. You're driving down the freeway in your car. Control, Influence, or Concern? Your car? Other drivers? Road conditions?

5. What you watch on TV.

6. What is available for you to watch on TV.

7. What your eight-year-old watches on Saturday morning while you're sleeping.

8. Whether or not your husband drinks alcohol to excess.

9. Whether or not you drink alcohol to excess.

10. Whether or not the neighbor four blocks away drinks alcohol to excess and drives by your house while you're backing out of your driveway.

11. Whether or not you get hit by this neighbor as you back out of your driveway.

12. Whether or not your parents got divorced.

13. Whether or not you get divorced.

14. Whether or not you get along well with your spouse.

15. Whether or not you say critical or contemptuous things to your spouse.

Answers:

1. Control. Your six-year-old can be physically removed from her bed. You may not be able to control whether or not she stands up afterwards, but you can control where she is.

2. Influence. You can control your language, offer rewards, etc., but unless you want to provoke a physical fight, you won't try for control.

3. Control. No one will push the ice cream down your throat—it is entirely up to you whether you eat it or not.

4. You control your own vehicle. You're concerned about other drivers and road conditions. You influence your safety by driving defensively, by watching both the other drivers and the road conditions, and by making necessary adjustments.

5. Control. The channel you watch is entirely up to you.

6. Concern. Broadcasters decide what is on TV. However, if you're a Nielsen Ratings family whose TV habits are monitored, you have a small amount of influence because surveys affect what is on TV.

7. Influence. Your training and your guidance will influence what your eight-year-old watches while you sleep. Of

course, if you're sleeping and haven't locked out certain channels, what your eight-year-old actually watches may be a concern.

8. Influence or Concern. The answer here depends on the individual situation. In some marriages, you might have some level of influence over your spouse's drinking. In most marriages, however, and in alcoholic situations in particular, it is best seen as concern.

9. Control. You make the choice.

10. Concern. You have to adjust to it, but you can't do anything about it.

11. Influence. Your level of influence depends on your attentiveness as you're backing out of the driveway. If you're looking around, you'll see your neighbor coming and wait to back out. If not, you're not adequately exerting your influence and may be hit.

12. Concern. Children do not control or even influence the parental decision to divorce, but they are usually affected deeply by that decision.

13. Influence. You and your spouse both have influence in the quality of your marriage and the likelihood of divorce. However, if one spouse decides unilaterally to divorce the other, then the divorce is in the control of that person while the other has little or no influence.

14. Influence. See above.

15. Control. What you say is your responsibility.

For most people, this insight is simple but extremely helpful. If you find that much of what you're reading here seems to apply to your own situation, the next step is to practice looking at the aspects and circumstances of your daily life, prayerfully considering which of the three categories best fits. Learning to do this will set you up for effectively moving from the Illusion of Control model to the Truth model. (Strategies for applying the Truth model will be discussed in the following chapters.)

Examining the situations of your life is also the first step in changing your assessment of yourself. Instead of being both the problem and the solution, which is the basis of the Illusion of Control, you begin to see yourself more truthfully. You're beginning to accept the fact that you *don't* control or even influence everything around you—precisely the situation you've been trying to ignore or deny all these years!

Of course, this will increase your discomfort at first! It feels unpredictable and might cause some anxiety. It's at this point, though, that you're beginning to challenge yourself to give up well-practiced solutions and risk changing to new strategies. As a poster in my office hallway states,

**The truth will set you free—
but first it will make you miserable!**

In many cases, people don't want to accept the fact that painful, hurtful, or bad events can happen to them and those around them—and that, humanly speaking, there may be nothing they can do. Fortunately, we're not talking in this book about what is only humanly possible. Instead, we're asking, "What is possible with God?" That's where we'll focus in the next chapter.

One final note. You might have noticed that I've discussed three categories thus far but the diagram has four compartments. What is the empty one?

All of us are surrounded by circumstances that are so far removed from our world and experience that, practically speaking, they have no emotional impact on us at all. Are you concerned about who the next Prime Minister of Sweden is going to be? Have you been following the changes in the price of tea in China? Do you have a bad day when the temperature in Calcutta never goes below 95 degrees? Some readers will say yes to one or more of these, but only because they have a personal stake or connection for some reason. For the rest of us, they don't even rate as our concern. We could label the fourth category *No Impact*.

For most Americans, terrorist attacks occurring overseas used to be something we were vaguely aware of but caused us minimal emotional response. On September 11, 2001, terrorism moved from the empty space on my diagram (No Impact) to the Concern category within a few minutes. Now we're forced to believe that it could, indeed has happened here in America. For those in the government and the military, it has moved from Concern to Influence as they try to make the right decisions to reduce the likelihood of another attack. Whatever your views on the strategies that have been employed, that is the nature of the situation we live in now. It also forces us to consider, "Where is God in all this?"

Chapter 9

———✦———

As we noted earlier in the Illusion of Control model, God is often seen as part of the world that the person controls (at least to some degree). Of course, few Christians would actually say, "Sure, I control what God does all that time." Yet it's not uncommon to find Christians who view their behavior as primary in predicting and controlling how God will act in their lives and circumstances. When someone is living in the Illusion of Control, they'll say things such as:

- "God won't bless me if I don't do my quiet time regularly."

- "I'm not that good of a Christian, so God won't hear my prayers."

- "I'm not like _____ (fill in the blank with the name of a popular Christian), so I'm sure God doesn't care about me."

- "I'm not doing enough for God, so He's probably mad at me."

- "I'm suffering because of difficulties in my life. I must be doing something wrong."

We all know that doing good is preferable to not doing good. And we know that there is often a relationship between success and doing good—consider the message found in the biblical book of Proverbs. But to draw a clear line of Control from a good deed performed in our youth to a specific, positive event that occurs as cause-and-effect when we're an adult is at best unlikely.

So where does God fit in the Truth model? If you'll look at the diagram on page 38, you'll see that God is clearly included.

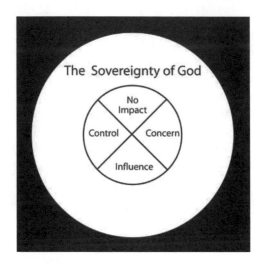

Scripture assures us that God is sovereign—that is, He rules over the entire universe, all of history, and all of us. For example:

> *For the Lord is the great God,*
> *the great King above all gods.*
> *In his hand are the depths of the earth,*
> *and the mountain peaks belong to him.*
> *The sea is his, for he made it,*
> *and his hands formed the dry land (Psalm 95:3-5).*

God tells Jeremiah,
> *"Before I formed you in the womb I knew you,*
> *before you were born I set you apart;*
> *I appointed you as a prophet to the nations"*
> *(Jeremiah 1:5).*

The entire content of Psalm 104 is a description of the sovereignty of God:

Praise the Lord, O my soul.
O Lord my God, you are very great;
you are clothed with splendor and majesty.
He wraps himself in light as with a garment;
he stretches out the heavens like a tent
and lays the beams of his upper chambers on their waters.
He makes the clouds his chariot and rides on the wings of
*   the wind.*
He makes winds his messengers, flames of fire his servants.
He set the earth on its foundations; it can never be moved.
You covered it with the deep as with a garment; the waters
*   stood above the mountains.*
But at your rebuke the waters fled, at the sound of your
*   thunder they took to flight;*
they flowed over the mountains, they went down into
*   the valleys,*
to the place you assigned for them.
You set a boundary they cannot cross; never again will they
*   cover the earth.*
He makes springs pour water into the ravines; it flows
*   between the mountains.*
They give water to all the beasts of the field; the wild
*   donkeys quench their thirst.*
The birds of the air nest by the waters;
they sing among the branches.
He waters the mountains from his upper chambers;
the earth is satisfied by the fruit of his work.
He makes grass grow for the cattle,
and plants for man to cultivate—
bringing forth food from the earth:
wine that gladdens the heart of man, oil to make his
*   face shine,*
and bread that sustains his heart.

The trees of the Lord are well watered, the cedars of
    Lebanon that he planted.
There the birds make their nests; the stork has its home in
    the pine trees.
The high mountains belong to the wild goats; the crags are
    a refuge for the coneys.
The moon marks off the seasons, and the sun knows when
    to go down.
You bring darkness, it becomes night, and all the beasts of
    the forest prowl.
The lions roar for their prey and seek their food from God.
The sun rises, and they steal away; they return and lie
    down in their dens.
Then man goes out to his work, to his labor until evening.
How many are your works, O Lord!
In wisdom you made them all; the earth is full of your
    creatures.
There is the sea, vast and spacious, teeming with creatures
    beyond number—living things both large and small.
There the ships go to and fro, and the leviathan, which
    you formed to frolic there.
These all look to you to give them their food at the
    proper time.
When you give it to them, they gather it up;
when you open your hand, they are satisfied with
    good things.
When you hide your face, they are terrified;
when you take away their breath, they die and return
    to the dust.
When you send your Spirit, they are created,
and you renew the face of the earth.
May the glory of the Lord endure forever;
may the Lord rejoice in his works—
he who looks at the earth, and it trembles,
who touches the mountains, and they smoke.

I will sing to the Lord all my life;
I will sing praise to my God as long as I live.
May my meditation be pleasing to him, as I rejoice in the
Lord.
But may sinners vanish from the earth and the wicked be
no more.
Praise the Lord, O my soul.
Praise the Lord (Psalm 104:1-35).

The Truth diagram tries to capture this *truth* in a visual way by putting our human world within the larger circle of God's sovereignty. This reminds us that while we must pay close attention to those things in our life, we are limited in what we are able to do or understand. Yet God is not limited. The diagram also allows us to describe visually the relationship between these areas of life (things we control, things we influence, and things that concern us) and the truth and fact of God's sovereignty. Specifically, it will allow us to look at the connection between our world and God: prayer.

Let's look first at those things we control. Recall that these include our tongue, our choice of what to eat or do, whether we arise at the sound of our alarm clock or decide to stay in bed a while longer. There are some of the things that no one else can do for us, and for which we are responsible. Jesus talked of one such example in Matthew 15:10–11.

Jesus called the crowd to him and said, "Listen and understand. What goes into a man's mouth does not make him 'unclean,' but what comes out of his mouth, that is what makes him 'unclean.'"

According to Jesus, we are responsible for what we say, and when bad things come out, it makes us unclean.

We also know from Paul's writing in Romans 6–8 that because of our sinful nature, the things for which we are responsible (according to the Law of God) are the very things we often do not do. Indeed, if we're not in Christ and have not been made *a new creation*, Paul says we're not able to do what the Law requires. Even as Christians, we know we fall down daily. We sin and need repentance and forgiveness. But for those for whom Jesus is not Lord and Savior, the power is lacking to truly please God.

This means that if you, the reader, are not committed to Jesus Christ as Lord and Savior, now would be an excellent time to explore what this means.

In his book, *What Your Counselor Never Told You,* Dr. William Backus summarizes it this way:

> God alone can and does defeat sin and its ability to control and damn us. This He did by an act more awesome than the prowess of evil. God actually became one of us and took upon Himself the role of condemned sinner; He adopted the task of defeating sin's power by dying under the penalty that was rightfully ours. By so doing, He set us free from sin—**from the guilt and punishment of sin and from the control over us of sin's power** (p. 37).[3]

The key phrase here is "from the control over us of sin's power." Later Dr. Backus concludes:

> We also learn that if we receive Him as our own answer, He will do what no psychologist, psychiatrist, professor, physicist, philosopher, or politician—no human being, including ourselves—can ever do. He will give us absolute triumph over sin's power and its consequences.

If you have not received Jesus Christ as Lord and Savior, consider doing that now. Then determine to pursue a relationship with Him. Otherwise, you're trying to do something that humans simply are not able to do on their own. Wouldn't it be worth your while? After all, only with God's help can we ever hope to lead normal, happy lives.

Dear Lord God,
   I understand full well that I am a sinner in need of a
Savior. I thank you for sending your Son, Jesus Christ, to show
us your grace and mercy, to teach us about your Kingdom, to
die on the cross for all of humanity, and be raised victorious
from the dead.
   Today I accept your free gift of grace. I accept Jesus as my
Lord and my Savior. I place on Him all the sins I have ever
committed, and I thank you for the cleansing and forgiveness
that you have promised those who put their trust in you.
   Now help me to go forward—walking daily in your love
and in the Truth of your Word. Connect me with godly people
that will be encouraging, healing, and instructive to me.
Above all, help me to understand the Truth about the Illusion
of Control so I can be victorious in this area of my life. I've
been in bondage for so long!
   Lord, I cannot live the abundant life without your
help, so I choose to trust in you completely. Only you can bring
me the freedom and joy I so desperately need. Thanking and
praising you in advance for what you'll accomplish in me,
I pray in Jesus' name. Amen.

Now let's continue our discussion of the first area: those things
that we *can* control.

More About Control

The word *Control* has, in common usage and in some psychological circles, gotten a bad name of late. People are
described as being *control freaks* or having *control issues*. I want
to be quite clear what I mean by control in the context of this
book, in contrast to these more popular meanings.

In this book, the word *Control* is used for a precise meaning
that's more like the scriptural concept of self-control, although it
goes beyond that meaning as well. When we say we have control
in some situation, it means that all of the variables are under our

authority, power, and responsibility (again, from a human perspective).

For example, your brain is directly responsible for the contraction of muscles in arms and legs that allow you to eat, dress, get out of bed, etc. When you hold a hammer in your hand, you control where the head falls (based on my own experience, however, some of us need practice to improve our accuracy). Your brain, both language and motor centers, control the words that come out of your mouth. Even someone who blurts something out is responsible for what they've said. In all these instances, we are in control—whether we like it or not, and whether we're willing to acknowledge it or not.

In contrast, there are other areas of life over which we have influence, but not total control. It is here, I believe, that the misunderstanding or perhaps misapplication of the word *control* occurs.

We have Influence in areas of life where we're *one* of the variables in outcomes and events—but we're not the only variable. We may be the major, most important variable, or play only a very small part. Regardless, we do have some say in the outcome if we have Influence.

So, yes, we do have Influence over our children's behavior, our spouse's mood, what our students learn, and whether or not we catch anything when we're fishing. But in each of these cases, there are other things that are contributing to the outcome as well.

Here are some examples. As parents, we can be brilliant and consistent, but some of our children's behavior is determined by their genetics, their gender, and the influence of other people. They also have a will of their own! I may offer my spouse my most loving behavior, but if they happened to lose their job that day, I may not appear to have much Influence at all. Likewise, excellent teachers can influence students to learn, but there will always be several confounding variables in the outcome of learning: some students will work harder than others, some will have a natural aptitude for the subject matter while others won't, students may show up at school unable to function well due to improper nutrition. Finally, as any good fisherman knows, when you fail to catch anything, the proper explanation is not, "I didn't know what I was doing." Rather, the accepted reason is always, "They just weren't biting out there today!"

Given the nature of Influence, we can make an important observation: when it comes to Influence in the context of relationships, the question is not always, "How can I be influential?" but rather, "How can I be influential and still maintain a solid relationship?"

As Christians, we're exhorted to "speak the truth in love" as a way to accomplish this. Unfortunately, we don't always make *relationship* a priority when we try to influence other people. Thus, when someone exerts influence in a relationship without regard to maintaining the health of that relationship, that person is described as controlling. I believe that in the popular jargon of our day, this is what people are really talking about when they refer to control or control issues: **exerting influence while damaging relationships.**

Let me give you an example. I may get immediate results if I yell at one of my children to do something around the house, but they're not going to feel emotionally connected to me in a positive way. If a man continually threatens his wife with physical violence, she may do what he tells her but the relationship will be seriously damaged. Even more subtle ways of influencing, such as sarcasm, emotional withdrawal, or simply ignoring the other person, may gain some influence but the cost will be paid by the relationship.

Personally, I find it more useful to focus my attention on helping people understand influence in a good way rather than to get into semantics. The word *control* is too imprecise and loaded with negative connotations to be helpful or truly descriptive. Indeed, in looking over a variety of articles on the concept of control, I was struck by the lack of any coherent or consistent definition of what the term really means.

Here is one example.

Controlling behavior:
behavior intended to control your own feelings,
Control how people feel about you and treat you,
Or control the outcome of things (Margaret Paul, Ph.D).[4]

This is very imprecise. Dr. Paul's definition includes both healthy and unhealthy behaviors. If I can tell myself the truth about a situation and thereby control my feelings, that's a good thing. If I go to a job interview and dress carefully to fit that situation, I'm trying to control people's first impression of me. Is that a bad thing? If I drive down the freeway and pay close attention to the cars around me, I'm trying to control the outcome—that is, I'm trying to arrive safely at my destination. Again, I would argue that this is a good thing.

I believe what Dr. Paul is really trying to address is either
1) exerting influence without regard to relationship, or
2) confusing control with influence—as defined by our model.

Either way, I think the language of control in the popular usage and in some professional contexts is not particularly helpful.

Control and Influence are two of our three categories. The third category is Concern. As I stated earlier, things in this category have an impact on our lives in some way, but they are not within our control or influence. An example would be the weather in Minnesota: we have to make adjustments to cope with it but that's all we can do, humanly speaking.

There are numerous examples in Scripture that remind human beings of their place in the world. When Job questions God, the Lord reminds Job of the many things He controls that are only *concerns* for human beings (see Job 40 and 41).

Job finally concludes:

> "I know that you can do all things;
> no plan of yours can be thwarted.
> You asked, 'Who is this that obscures my counsel without
>   knowledge?'
> Surely I spoke of things I did not understand,
> things too wonderful for me to know" (Job 42:1-3).

Jesus reminds us that we can worry but we can't add a day to our lives by doing so. He asks, "Who of you by worrying can add a single hour to his life?" (Luke 12:25).

And in Romans, Paul reminds us that our sinful condition is something only Jesus Christ can deal with. According to Romans 3:23, all of us have sinned and fall short of the glory of God. It is vitally important that we understand this truth and are realistic about those things that are merely concerns. Trying to control or influence things that are concerns is a recipe for frustration and a feeling of failure.

Chapter 10

Let's take another look at the diagram:

We're trying to grasp the relationship between those things in our lives that might be called *human-oriented* and those things that are *God-oriented*. Control, Influence, and Concern describe aspects of our human experience and are therefore human-oriented. Those things that exist within the larger reality of God's sovereignty in the world are God-oriented. What is it, then, that connects these two parts—these two orientations?

The first is the guidance of the Holy Spirit through the gifts of discernment, wisdom, and knowledge. Guidance helps us understand the difference between those things in our lives we can Control, those we can Influence, and those that are only Concerns. It is essential that we get the Lord's perspective on these things and truly grasp the Truth as it applies to our lives. To mistakenly categorize a particular situation, person, behavior, or problem is to apply a faulty or failing solution. Just as a doctor needs to know whether you have a viral or a bacterial infection in order to prescribe the correct treatment, we need to be clear in the diagnosis of our difficulties.

So our first connection between the *human*-orientation and the *God*-orientation is this: we need to ask for guidance and clarity in our diagnosis. "Is this an area of Control, where I have total responsibility? Is this an area of Influence, where I have some say in the outcome but must apply my influence wisely? Or must I accept the fact that I have absolutely no say in this matter, humanly speaking, and therefore am dealing with an area of Concern?"

Praying for wisdom and discernment is the first way we connect the human and the spiritual, or the human-orientation with the God-orientation. Here is a sample prayer:

> *Father God, Creator and Lord of the Universe, I acknowledge that your ways are not my ways, and my thoughts are not your thoughts. Help me understand my responsibility in this situation:*
>
> _____
>
> _____
>
> _____
>
> *I express my willingness to take responsibility for the areas of Control and Influence, and I release my areas of Concern to you. By your Holy Spirit, guide me, direct me, and give me the gifts of wisdom, knowledge, and discernment in this situation. In Jesus' name I pray, Amen.*

Then we need to listen and reflect, anticipating that we will receive clarity and direction from God on the matter. Once we're clear on which area we're operating in, we can continue to connect the human and the spiritual through prayer. But just as a doctor applies the proper treatment to a viral or bacterial infection, we need to apply the proper *prayer treatment* to each of our situations. That is our next subject.

Look again at the diagram as we consider the area of Control. Remember that humanly speaking, this area is totally your own responsibility. No one else is involved—they can't help, and they can't be blamed!

Because of our fallen, fallible state, however, we need to acknowledge that even though we are responsible for something, we often fail. We use our tongues to speak evil (sinful things) rather than blessing and truth. We know we shouldn't eat more dessert, but we choose the unwise path anyway. We drive faster than we should because we're late for an appointment. It's often our responsibility when someone else gets hurt. The local constable pulls us over and gives us another responsibility: pay a ticket or go to jail.

So what is it that we need?

For starters, we need to ask the Lord for more of the fruit of the Spirit. In particular, we need the fruit of self-control. We also need to ask for forgiveness for past mistakes, and ask for wisdom to avoid the same in the future. *"Lead us not into temptation, but deliver us from evil"* is one way this is expressed in the Lord's Prayer. In Romans 6–8, Paul talks in detail about struggling in the area of Control, declaring at one point in Romans 7:24-25, *"What a wretched man I am! Who will rescue me from this body of death? Thanks be to God—through Jesus Christ our Lord!"*

Yes, we need deliverance from our flesh's tendency to be irresponsible and sinful so we can live by the Spirit. Here is a sample prayer:

> *Lord Jesus, I acknowledge that I have sometimes been irresponsible in areas that are fully my own responsibility. I will not say I have no sin. Instead, as John called me to do, I now confess my sin to you in the following areas:*
>
> _____
>
> _____
>
> _____
>
> _____
>
> *As your Word promises, I receive your forgiveness for this sin. Cleanse me from my unrighteousness. I also ask, Lord, for wisdom and discernment in the future so I can avoid falling into temptation or being lazy, slothful, or irresponsible. Grow in me the fruit of your Holy Spirit, especially that of self-control. I want to please you by taking charge of those things over which I truly have control. By doing so, I can be a good steward of the gifts and responsibilities you have given me. In Jesus' name I pray, Amen.*

To sum up: we need the help of the Lord to accurately identify which areas of our lives are truly under our Control, and in praying about these areas, we need to ask for wisdom, self-control, and a willingness to take on the proper responsibility.

Influence has some things in common with Control, particularly in the ways in which we need help from God. As before, we need the Spirit to guide us into Truth so we can identify those areas in which we truly have influence. This is the first connection between us and God's sovereign role.

In addition to determining if something is within our realm of Influence, we need to be clear about the level or amount of influence we actually have. For example, if my six-year-old daughter doesn't want to go to bed, I can physically pick her up and place her there. I can influence her behavior and apply consequences if she gets out of bed again. However, I have little influence over whether she actually falls asleep or not. I can turn out the lights except for a night light, make sure she has enough covers, and maybe turn on a music tape to help her relax. Beyond those efforts, she'll go to sleep when she's ready, regardless of what I want. Concerning my 16-year-old son, I'd be hard-pressed to physically place him in bed if he didn't want to be there. I'm limited to explaining the consequences or setting up reinforcers. My prior experience as his parent will dictate how (or if) I enforce obedience to my rules and requests.

As we discuss the concept of Influence, something I find interesting is that right away in the book of Genesis, God, the Creator of the Universe, chooses to limit Himself to having only Influence in the lives of His people—not Control. He preferred that human beings would have a *choice* to love, worship, and obey Him. If God were in total Control of our activities and behavior, all of us would resemble robots or marionettes, and our responses would be programmed—based on Him pulling the right strings at the right time. It would be the appearance of free will and choice, but it would be an Illusion.

We need the Lord to help us identify our areas of Influence, to be clear about the amount of influence we actually have, and to use our influence wisely and effectively.

Earlier, I discussed the popular concept of Control and redefined it as "exerting influence without regard to relationship." This is reflected in God's interaction with human beings. Above all, He desires relationship. Only in the most extreme circumstances will He let people withdraw from Him or choose to rebel. He does not use His influence to damage relationship—only to maintain it whenever possible.

Throughout Scripture, we see God's use of Influence to bring His people back to Him. The Judges and the Prophets in the Old Testament were God's representatives, calling Israel back to Him. Later on, the purpose of Jesus' coming to earth to teach, heal, and go to the cross was so God could exert Influence in His relationship with humanity. He did this by offering salvation through the sacrifice of Jesus, who paid the price for our sin.

This still was not Control on God's part. It's still possible for human beings to reject even this free offer of salvation by grace through faith. But it was the ultimate solution to the distance between God and humanity that was and is created by sin. In Christ, God was exerting maximum Influence on us without damaging the relationship.

Here is a sample prayer that illustrates how we might approach God for help in the area of our Influence:

Father God, I thank you that in your grace, mercy, and wisdom, you have exerted your influence throughout history in order to restore the relationship between yourself and the world. I am personally grateful that you sent your Son to be the sacrifice for my sin. You opened the door to a relationship with you and the promise of eternal life. As a thankful response to you, I express my desire to understand my areas of Influence. Help me to accurately identify those areas in which I have Influence. Show me what they are and how much influence I actually have. Then please help me understand how to exert that Influence in a kind, loving, and gracious way so as to not damage my relationships. If I have tried to Influence others in a way that is damaging to them or our relationship, open my heart to the illumination of your Holy Spirit. Show me and then convict me that I might repent of this and change my approach to these people. Give me wisdom, self-control, mercy, and skill in my areas of Influence for Jesus' sake, Amen.

When we think things through under the guidance of the Holy Spirit, we will also discover (sometimes to our dismay, sometimes to our great relief) that in our world there are many, many things over which we have neither Control nor Influence. They are Concerns. I'm defining areas of Concern as those things in our world and experience that affect us in some way, large or small, but over which we have absolutely no effect, humanly speaking.

Unfortunately, all too often we make one of several mistakes when it comes to Concerns. First, we may deny that we have no say and try desperately to make some sort of change.

Trying to solve problems when we're dealing in the area of Concern makes us discouraged and frustrated because we're doomed to failure. What we tend to do, however, is get anxious about these things. In a sense, when we fret and worry and brood and ruminate about things in this category, we're operating under this subtle misbelief: *worrying does something.*

The problem is, worrying about things over which we have neither Influence nor Control does not help at all. Still, in contrast, there are times when fear that is based on Truth causes us to take Control or exert our Influence in an effort to increase our safety. We fear getting thrown through our windshield so we use our seat belt. We fear food poisoning so we handle our meat carefully and cook it fully. In these cases, we have some level of Control or Influence, and taking action on that basis is useful and wise. Simply worrying *without* taking action, however, is what we do when things are Concerns, since by definition, there is no action that will help.

Fortunately, Scripture has an excellent strategy for dealing with this problem. That is our next topic.

Chapter 11

—⊂≡≡≡≡⊃—

To understand how to effectively deal with areas of Concern, we need to briefly retrace the life of Paul. He gives us our strategy here.

We remember that Paul was converted through his Damascus road experience (Acts 9). He then spends the rest of his life bringing the gospel of Jesus Christ to the Gentiles, who were the non-Jews in the known world. During this time he had many instances of great trial and suffering. He summarizes them in 2 Corinthians.

I repeat: Let no one take me for a fool. But if you do, then receive me just as you would a fool, so that I may do a little boasting. In this self-confident boasting I am not talking as the Lord would, but as a fool. Since many are boasting in the way the world does, I too will boast. You gladly put up with fools since you are so wise! In fact, you even put up with anyone who enslaves you or exploits you or takes advantage of you or pushes himself forward or slaps you in the face. To my shame I admit that we were too weak for that!

What anyone else dares to boast about—I am speaking as a fool—I also dare to boast about. Are they Hebrews? So am I. Are they Israelites? So am I. Are they Abraham's descendants? So am I. Are they servants of Christ? (I am out of my mind to talk like this.) I am more. I have worked much harder, been in prison more frequently, been flogged more severely, and been exposed to death again and again. Five times I received from the Jews the forty lashes minus one. Three times I was beaten with rods, once I was stoned, three times I was shipwrecked, I spent a night and a day in the open sea, I have been constantly on the move. I have been in danger from rivers, in danger from bandits, in danger from my own countrymen, in danger from Gentiles; in danger in the city, in danger in the country, in danger at sea; and in danger from false brothers. I have labored and toiled and have often gone without sleep; I have known hunger and thirst and have often gone without food; I have been cold and naked. Besides everything else, I face daily the pressure of my concern for all the churches. Who is weak, and I do not feel weak? Who is led into sin, and I do not inwardly burn?

If I must boast, I will boast of the things that show my weakness. The God and Father of the Lord Jesus, who is to be praised forever, knows that I am not lying. In Damascus the governor under King Aretas had the city of the Damascenes guarded in order to arrest me. But I was lowered in a basket from a window in the wall and slipped through his hands (2 Corinthians 11:16-33).

Here is a summary of what Paul went through:

- Five times he received 39 lashes.
- Three times he was beaten with rods.
- Once he was stoned.
- Three times he was shipwrecked.
- Once he spent a day and night in the open sea.
- He had gone without sleep.
- He had been hungry and thirsty.
- He had been cold and naked.

- He escaped the King of Damascus by being lowered in a basket.

- He was constantly in danger.

- Through all this, he had concern for the churches he'd established.

Let's try to imagine a life like Paul's as we consider our own response to our areas of Concern. The passage we're going to examine was written by the man who experienced these things and more in the course of his ministry. Paul isn't approaching the subject academically or from a safe distance when he writes about how he handled trials, the things out of his Control and Influence. Instead, he writes in the context of his personal, extreme suffering.

The passage we're focusing on is one of the relatively few *How-To* texts in the New Testament. It's important because Paul wrote it from Rome, where he was imprisoned at the end of his life. He wrote this to a church that he'd started and to people that he dearly loved. That means we can look at it as a culmination of Paul's life experience of training in the Lord.

> *Rejoice in the Lord always. I will say it again: Rejoice!*
> *Let your gentleness be evident to all. The Lord is near.*
> *Do not be anxious about anything, but in everything,*
> *by prayer and petition, with thanksgiving, present your*
> *requests to God. And the peace of God, which tran-*
> *scends all understanding, will guard your hearts and*
> *your minds in Christ Jesus* (Philippians 4:4-7).

> *Finally, brothers, whatever is true, whatever is noble,*
> *whatever is right, whatever is pure, whatever is lovely,*
> *whatever is admirable—if anything is excellent or*
> *praiseworthy—think about such things. Whatever you*
> *have learned or received or heard from me, or seen in*
> *me—put it into practice. And the God of peace will be*
> *with you* (Philippians 4:8-9).

Unless we already knew about the trials Paul had experienced, it would be easy to dismiss his words. How would you like someone who's comfortable and free of worries telling you, "Don't be anxious about anything!" We would find it annoying. But when Paul speaks, we listen differently. We're not just getting a lecture on how not to be anxious, we're getting his own tried and true approach to trials—things he learned from the Lord through the hours and hours he spent in pain and suffering during situations that were totally out of his Influence or Control. In other words, what we have in this short passage is Paul's answer to our question: "How do I handle my areas of Concern?"

Let's take a closer look at what Paul tells us to do. His instructions come in two parts. Part one is found in verses 4-7, and part two is found in verses 8-9.

...by prayer. The meaning of the Greek word used here includes prayer addressed to God along with places where one might pray. It's used in Scripture for times of prayer that are very intentional, set aside for a purpose. In 1 Corinthians, Paul uses the word again when he tells husbands and wives not to withhold sexual intimacy from one another except for a season when they would devote themselves to prayer. Jesus uses it to describe the temple as a place (house) of prayer. Paul is using the word here as a time set aside in which focused, specific prayer is done.

...petition. Coming from a position of need or want, this is a seeking, asking, or entreating for help from God. It's used in other passages for the kind of prayer that expresses a specific need or want, either for the person praying or on behalf of someone else.

...with thanksgiving. This is fairly obvious. When we read other Scriptures, though, it becomes clear that this is much more than the attitude of our heart when we approach God in prayer. It's being thankful for the opportunity to even do so. It's also the anticipation of what He will do, and the many things He has already done for us.

...present your requests to God. The focus here is on the specific things we're asking of God. We're encouraged to actually let Him know what it is that we want or need.

Taken together, we get a picture of someone who comes to God for a specific, focused time of prayer. During this period, the person is aware of a particular need that could cause, or is causing, anxiety. She comes with an attitude of thanksgiving—maybe even calling to mind specific things she's thankful for and giving glory to God for those things.

Finally, she makes her requests known, putting them before God until she has a sense of being *done*. Her sense of completion is indicated by the final promise in this passage—the peace of God, which transcends her understanding, keeps her heart and mind safe in Christ Jesus.

What's interesting from a psychological point of view is what comes next. Once all our prayers and thanksgivings are finished, it would be easy to start thinking about the Concerns again. Can you see how that would be? After focusing on the problem in prayer, how do you suddenly stop thinking about it? Sometimes we like to tell people to, "Let go and let God," or "Just give it to Jesus." Unfortunately, our thoughts don't function like items that can be given away and left there. Thoughts are more like dandelions: you can give them to your neighbor, but they still seem to want to grow in your back yard!

So Paul (after lots of practice, no doubt) gives us another part of the strategy. Look at the second portion again:

> *Finally, brothers, whatever is true, whatever is noble, whatever is right, whatever is pure, whatever is lovely, whatever is admirable—anything is excellent or praiseworthy—think about such things. Whatever you have learned or received or heard from me, or seen in me— put it into practice. And the God of peace will be with you* (Philippians 4:8-9).

Paul has discovered, no doubt over many hours of very lonely time, a way to move from focusing on his Concerns to refocusing his mind and thoughts onto other things. Not simply letting go and letting God, but rather, intentionally, purposefully taking his thoughts in an entirely different direction. And he describes this technique in a way that can be personalized by anyone.

Rather than giving us specifics, Paul gives us categories. *Whatever is noble....* What comes to mind? Winston Churchill? A king? The color of nobility: purple? *Whatever is right....* My wife, Sherry, is always right. *Whatever is pure....* Clear cold water, new-fallen snow.

When we deliberately rehearse these kinds of things in our self-talk, it changes how we feel. Even during a shipwreck, or when recovering from a beating, Paul must have found that by doing this, he felt less anxious and more peaceful.

Here is a format for personalizing this tool and applying it to your own areas of Concern. Each step comes from a portion of Paul's writing and is followed by space where you can fill in the unique details that describe what you're anxious about and how you desire to bring these Concerns to the Lord.

Then you'll be asked to construct a list of positive things based on Paul's categories and what personally stimu-lates/encourages/brightens you. When you're done praying, move to this list as a way of focusing your attention on positive and encouraging things.

Facing My Trials with Philippians 4

"Rejoice in the Lord always.
I will say it again: Rejoice!
Let your gentleness be evident to all.
The Lord is near.
Do not be anxious about anything..."
(Philippians 4:4-6)

Lord, I acknowledge that I'm anxious about: _____

_____

_____

_____

_____

_____

_____

_____

_____

_____

"... but in everything, by prayer..."

Lord, my focus during this prayer time will be:

_____

_____

_____

_____

_____

_____

_____

_____

I'm aware of being in need in this way:

_____

_____

_____

_____

_____

_____

_____

_____

"...with thanksgiving..."

Lord, I'm thankful for:

_____

_____

_____

_____

_____

_____

_____

_____

_____

"...present your requests to God."

Father, these are my requests:

_____

_____

_____

_____

_____

_____

_____

_____

_____

_____

"And the peace of God, which transcends all understanding, will guard your hearts and your minds in Christ Jesus."

• • • •

And now, Lord, help me to re-direct my thoughts.

"Whatever is true..." makes me think of:

_____

_____

_____

_____

_____

_____

_____

_____

_____

_____

"Whatever is noble..." reminds me of:

_____

_____

_____

_____

_____

_____

_____

_____

_____

"Whatever is right..." makes me think of:

_____

_____

_____

_____

_____

_____

_____

_____

_____

"Whatever is pure..." I'm thinking about:

_____
_____
_____
_____
_____
_____
_____
_____
_____

"Whatever is lovely..." reminds me of:

_____
_____
_____
_____
_____
_____
_____
_____
_____

"Whatever is admirable..." makes me think of:

_____
_____
_____
_____
_____
_____
_____
_____
_____

"If anything is excellent or praiseworthy..." I'm thinking about:

_____
_____
_____
_____
_____
_____
_____
_____
_____
_____

"Think on these things!"

Chapter 12

————✦————

Many of us struggle with the results of living our lives under the Illusion of Control. By acknowledging both how appealing it can be and how devastating its effects usually are, we can begin to make changes in our beliefs and in our lives. When we choose to change our *model* of the world, give up the Illusion of Control, and embrace the Truth, we begin the healing process.

Little by little, as we effectively and consistently apply the Truth to our situations, we're able to take responsibility for those things that are under our Control and Influence. At the same time, we learn to recognize and release those things that in reality are only Concerns.

Another benefit of learning to deal with the Illusion of Control is that we become able over time to see the way in which God sovereignly relates to us in our human experience. With that understanding, our prayer life can become clearer and more focused on what is really needed in the situations we face.

So, whatever happened to Margie? I'm happy to report that not only did she finish graduate school and receive her license in Marriage and Family Therapy, but she's now in private practice helping others. Married to a pastor, she's a mother, stepmother, and grandmother several times over.

This is her reaction to reading *The Illusion of Control*:

> "Many times, even now, I find myself feeling an element of surprise when I hear another person sum-marize the unhealthy dynamics of my past. For so many years I'd bounced between my feelings of 'This is crazy—it doesn't make sense' and 'I'm crazy—because it appears to make sense to everyone else.' But either way, it was 'my normal.' (As a child, gut instinct often told me things weren't right and having an inquisitive

nature I was compelled to ask questions that were not welcomed by the family. They preferred to say words like, 'we're the best family' or 'thank God we're not like them,' and not look at how we really lived life—how the words and the reality didn't mesh. They bought into perhaps who they wanted to be, rather than who they were.) Ultimately, I suppose, to fit in at some level I landed in a place of believing that it was my problem since I was the only one in the family who didn't seem to 'get it.' In a crazy sort of way, placing myself at the center of the problem was the only thing that gave me even a modicum of control.

"If it was their issue—there was little, if anything, I could do about it. But, if I could find a way to 'own' the problem, then there was hope—hope that I could find a solution that could change the way life felt.

"In spite of that self-talk, my emotional being could never quite buy into it fully. Every time life hit a really rough spot, I would find myself sinking into a depression, battling between what I felt was truth and the truth others were conveying to me. But, as Steve Wiese stated in *The Illusion of Control*, there almost always comes a time in life when the Illusion no longer works. It was such an event in my life that left me scrambling for truth. That event felt like such a personal tragedy, it would not allow me to buy into the 'family talk' any longer. My mind hit search mode and would not shut down. I scrambled to try and find a way to take ownership of the problem so that I could DO something about it, but I couldn't pretend to buy into the family mindset any longer. That was when we began the process that uncovered the Illusion.

"As I read through *The Illusion of Control*, I felt an onslaught of emotions. I suppose it sounds funny to say, but even though I've spent years coming to understand the dynamics in my family of origin, it is rare that

I've looked at the overall picture in kind of a snapshot way. For years I had felt responsible for creating count-less pain within my family, and I had come to believe I was responsible for the events that had created that pain. If I had just not asked my questions—if I could have just bought in like the rest—life would have/could have been different. Those were painful years when I felt that no one really knew my heart and I suppose because they didn't, I doubted it myself. Now, reading 'Margie's' story woven throughout *The Illusion of Control*, I felt known. Perhaps because it provided that kind of a snapshot look, it was a rare moment where I felt understood and accepted, not just for who I am today, but for my past experiences.

"God, being God, used the very thing that got me into trouble (my inquisitive nature) to help me find truth. At the core, I am a truth-seeker. No matter how painful that may be, truth is what dictates my thoughts, my choices, my life in general. Ultimately, that meant surrendering to God and allowing Him His rightful place in my life. Placing my focus on Christ and run-ning life through that filter, rather than my clouded filter, is the only thing that allowed me to continue placing one foot in front of the other.

"It is my prayer that *The Illusion of Control* will be a tool for others, as it was for me, to accept those areas of your life over which you have no control, and to take charge of the areas that you do."

If you were to talk with Margie, she'd tell you that her strug-gle against the Illusion of Control will probably never be com-pletely over. Whenever stress levels are high, when she's taking on new challenges, or when life for some reason is being painful or difficult, she still has a tendency to go back and see *herself* as the problem. The difference now, though, is that she knows she has to battle the Illusion of Control by clinging to the Truth.

ADDITIONAL RESOURCES

Sometimes additional resources can be helpful to use in our healing and growth process. If you want to more fully understand *Misbelief Therapy*, the foundation this work is based upon, you can choose from several books by Dr. William Backus, including *Telling Yourself the Truth, Learning to Tell Myself the Truth, The Good News About Worry*, and *The Hidden Rift With God*. These books can be found at your local Christian Bookstore or can be ordered through The Center for Christian Psychological Services, 2780 Snelling Avenue North, Suite #104, St. Paul, Minnesota 55113.

Another good book is *Search for Significance* by Robert McGee.[5] He addresses the tendency to evaluate our worth on the basis of our performance and other people's opinions very well. There are, of course, many other good books that can support us in our quest for health and healing. Most are available at Christian Bookstores or even online.

Again, my thanks to Margie for being willing to be included in this book. It's a testament to the fact that she desperately wants others to know the Truth so they, too, can be freed from the bondage that comes with the Illusion of Control. Over time, Margie learned there are no guarantees—life can be both difficult or painful. But she's come to realize that facing the pain of life is better than operating out of an *illusion* that leads only to depression and anxiety.

My earnest hope and prayer is that this material will also help you in your walk into wholeness and freedom. And may the Lord bless you in your efforts!

Steven Wiese
St. Paul, Minnesota

Recommended Reading

Dr. William Backus, *What Your Counselor Never Told You: Seven Secrets Revealed—Conquer the Power of Sin in Your Life.* Paperback, 250 pages, Baker Publishing Group. ISBN-10: 0764223925, ISBN-13: 978-0764223921

Dr. William Backus, *Telling Yourself the Truth.* Paperback, 224 pages, Bethany House Publishers. ISBN-10: 0764223259, ISBN-13: 978-0764223259

Dr. William Backus, *Learning to Tell Myself the Truth.* Paperback, 224 pages, Bethany House Publishers. ISBN-10: 1556612907, ISBN-13: 978-1556612909

Dr. William Backus, *The Good News About Worry.* Paperback, 219 pages, Bethany House Publishers. ISBN-10: 1556611870, ISBN-13: 978-1556611872

Dr. William Backus, *The Hidden Rift With God.* Paperback, 192 pages, Bethany House Publishers. ISBN-10: 1556610971, ISBN-13: 978-1556610974

Robert McGee, *Search for Significance.* Paperback: 352 pages, Thomas Nelson. ISBN-10: 0849944244, ISBN-13: 978-0849944246

Biography

Steven Wiese recently celebrated 22 years of marriage to his wife, Sherry. He and Sherry have five children. Since 1985, he has practiced psychology at the Center for Christian Psychological Services, founded by the late Dr. William Backus. Since 1996, he has served as Director of CCPS in addition to his private practice. He does individual and marriage and family therapy with older children, adolescents, and adults.

Steve began as a lay staff member at North Heights Lutheran Church in 1985, and during that time assisted Dr. Backus in the training and supervision of lay counselors, as well as some teaching and worship-leading duties.

Since 1992, he has served at North Heights as an Associate Pastor. Since 1991 he has served as the Director of the North Heights Counseling Clinic, which is currently staffed by 30 volunteer lay counselors. He is responsible for their training and supervision. In addition, he does preaching, teaching, staff consultation, and other pastoral duties as needed. He serves half-time.

Steve has taught/consulted with several other organizations on an occasional basis, including the World Mission Prayer League, the Lay Ministry Training Center, Masters' Institute, Presbyterian Homes, and Concordia Academy, a Lutheran High School located in St. Paul. In 1989, he taught the principles of Christian Counseling in Gothenburg, Sweden, and Hamburg, Germany, and in 1998 in Uppsala and Lund, Sweden.

Steve enjoys time with his family, hunting and fishing, photography and videography. He hopes someday to become the man his dog thinks he is.

EDUCATION
1976, BA, Gustavus Adolphus College, Magna Cum Laud,
Major in Psychology, Minor in Music
1976–77 — Bethel Seminary, M.Div. program
1978–79 — Orebromissionsskola, Orebro, Sweden, M.Div.
       program
1979–81 — M.S. University of Wisconsin-Madison, Counseling
       and Guidance
1983–86 — M.Div., Luther Northwestern Seminary

PROFESSIONAL CREDENTIALS
1984 — Licensed Psychologist in Minnesota
1992 — Ordained Lutheran Pastor

CONTACT INFORMATION
Steven R. Wiese
21211 Imperial Ave. N.
Forest Lake, MN 55025
651-464-1121
www.StevenWiese.com
www.TheIllusionofControl.com

NOTES

[1] Herbert Benson, M.D., with Miriam Z. Klipper, *The Relaxation Response*, 240 pages. Copyright 1975 by William Morrow & Company, Inc., HarperCollins Publishers. ISBN:0380815958

[2] John Gottman, *Clinical Manual for Marital Therapy—A Research-Based Approach*, p. 132. Copyright 2000 John Gottman, www.gottman.com

[3] Dr. William Backus, *What Your Counselor Never Told You: Seven Secrets Revealed—Conquer the Power of Sin in Your Life*. Paperback, 250 pages, Baker Publishing Group. ISBN-10: 0764223925, ISBN-13: 978-0764223921

[4] Margaret Paul, Ph.D., "Controlling Behavior? How Do You Attempt to Control," article, www.innerbonding.com.

[5] Robert McGee, *Search for Significance*. Paperback: 352 pages, Thomas Nelson. ISBN-10: 0849944244, ISBN-13: 978-0849944246